State Sovereignty's Shifting Sands

Reconciling state sovereignty with international criminal justice

Cecilia Hartwell

Contents

1 Introduction: The Shifting Landscape 5

1.1 Defining State Sovereignty 8

1.2 The Rise of International Justice 11

2 Historical Context: Sovereignty's Evolution . 15

2.1 Westphalian System and its limits 19

2.2 Emergence of International Law 22

2.3 Post-WWII Developments 25

3 International Criminal Court: Jurisdiction and Challenges 29

3.1 The ICC's Mandate 31

3.2 Complementarity Principle 34

3.3 State Cooperation & Obstacles 37

3.4 Criticisms and Reforms 40

3.5 Effectiveness Evaluation 43

4 National Sovereignty vs. Universal Jurisdiction 49

4.1 Defining Universal Jurisdiction 52

4.2 Conflicts and Tensions 56

5 Case Studies: Conflicts and Compromises . . 59
5.1 Rwanda Genocide Tribunal 62
5.2 Yugoslavia Tribunal 65
5.3 Contemporary Examples 69

6 The Future of International Criminal Justice 73
6.1 Strengthening the ICC 76
6.2 State Cooperation Strategies 79
6.3 Balancing Sovereignty and Justice 81

7 Conclusion: Towards a Harmonious Future . 85
7.1 Reconciliation Efforts 88
7.2 Looking Ahead 91

1 Introduction: The Shifting Landscape

State sovereignty, traditionally understood as the absolute authority of a state within its borders, faces increasing challenges in the 21st century. This inherent power, once unquestioned, is now frequently weighed against the burgeoning field of international criminal justice. The rise of global interconnectedness and the horrors of mass atrocities have driven the development of international legal mechanisms intended to hold individuals accountable for crimes that transcend national boundaries. This tension - between the long-held principle of state control and the imperative for international justice - forms the central theme of this exploration.

The historical evolution of this dynamic is complex. The Westphalian system, establishing the modern state system, prioritized state sovereignty above all else. It prioritized national self-determination and non-interference, a foundation that, while promoting stability, inherently limited the capacity for international intervention in matters of internal state affairs. However, the two

World Wars, with their unprecedented scale of human suffering, undeniably exposed the inadequacies of this system in preventing and punishing mass atrocities. The subsequent rise of international human rights law and the Nuremberg trials marked a pivotal shift, demonstrating a growing international consensus that certain crimes are so egregious they demand a response beyond national jurisdictions.

The establishment of the International Criminal Court (ICC) represents a significant milestone in this ongoing evolution. Its mandate to prosecute individuals for genocide, war crimes, crimes against humanity, and the crime of aggression reflects a determined effort to create a permanent and independent institution for international criminal justice. Yet, the ICC's operation is far from seamless. The principle of complementarity, designed to ensure the ICC only acts when national courts are unwilling or unable to genuinely prosecute, presents both practical and political challenges. Securing the cooperation of states, particularly those accused of perpetrating atrocities, remains a crucial yet often elusive goal. Furthermore, persistent criticisms of the Court's selectivity and potential bias necessitate ongoing evaluation and potential reforms. The ultimate effectiveness of the ICC, therefore, continues to be the subject of debate and scholarly analysis. A critical element of this ongoing reconciliation is universal jurisdiction. This principle grants national courts the power to prosecute individuals for serious international crimes, regardless of where the crime occurred or the nationality of the perpetrator or victim. While seemingly offering a powerful tool for accountability, universal jurisdiction also significantly challenges the established norms of state sovereignty. It inherently involves states exercising jurisdiction over individuals beyond their territorial boundaries, potentially leading to conflicts and tensions with states asserting their own sovereign prerogative to investigate and prosecute crimes. Managing this complex interplay requires delicate diplomatic negotiation and a clear understanding of the limitations and potential for abuse within the concept of universal jurisdiction.

Numerous case studies illustrate the practical complexities of navigating this terrain. The International Criminal Tribunal for Rwanda and the International Criminal Tribunal for the former Yugoslavia, while groundbreaking in their pursuit of justice, also exposed the difficulties inherent in prosecuting individuals for crimes committed during periods of widespread conflict and instability. These tribunals demonstrate that delivering justice while respecting state sovereignty often necessitates careful negotiation, compromise, and at times, considerable political maneuvering. The ongoing implications of these past tribunals, and the challenges faced by contemporary international justice mechanisms, serve to emphasize the evolving nature of these complex interplays.

The future of international criminal justice hinges on the ability to strengthen international institutions while simultaneously respecting the legitimate interests of sovereign states. This includes bolstering the ICC's capacity, promoting greater state cooperation through effective diplomatic engagement, and fostering a shared understanding of the crucial link between international accountability and the prevention of future atrocities. The path ahead necessitates continuous dialogue, compromise, and an unwavering commitment to both justice and the preservation of international order. Only through such a concerted effort can we achieve a world where state sovereignty and international criminal justice coexist, not as opposing forces, but as complementary elements in the pursuit of a just and peaceful global order. The challenge remains considerable, requiring innovative and flexible approaches to the complex realities of international relations. However, the imperative for accountability for the most egregious crimes against humanity remains paramount, demanding the continued pursuit of practical and workable solutions.

1.1 Defining State Sovereignty

State sovereignty, at its core, represents the supreme authority within a defined territory. This authority, traditionally understood, encompasses exclusive control over internal affairs, the ability to enter into international agreements, and independence from external interference. This classical definition, however, often clashes with the increasingly interconnected and globalized world we inhabit. The rise of international humanitarian law, for instance, has introduced limitations to the absolute nature of state power, particularly concerning the protection of human rights within their borders. The very essence of state sovereignty is challenged when a state fails to protect its own citizens from atrocities, leading to the rise of international mechanisms meant to address these failures.

The concept of sovereignty, historically rooted in the Peace of Westphalia, has undergone significant transformations. The Westphalian system, while establishing the principle of state equality and non-interference, failed to adequately address the issue of crimes against humanity, genocides, and other grave violations of international law. These crimes, by their very nature, transcend national borders and challenge the traditional notion of a state's exclusive jurisdiction over its own citizens. Consequently, the limitations of the Westphalian system become apparent, prompting the creation of international mechanisms to supplement, not replace, state sovereignty in dealing with crimes that affect the international community as a whole. The emergence of international human rights law and international criminal law serves to illustrate this evolution.

These developments have not been without their critics. Many states, particularly those who are frequently the subject of international scrutiny, view international criminal justice mechanisms as an infringement upon their hard-won sovereignty. Concerns about political motivations, double standards, and the potential for bias in international courts are often raised. It's a delicate balance; the desire to preserve state autonomy clashes with the imperative to prevent and punish the most heinous crimes against humanity. The challenge lies in finding a framework where states retain considerable autonomy while simultaneously acknowledging their responsibility to uphold universally recognized human rights standards and cooperate in the pursuit of global justice. This tension is particularly evident in the debates surrounding the International Criminal Court (ICC). The ICC, while lauded by many as a significant step towards global justice, faces considerable obstacles. The principle of complementarity, aiming to avoid duplication of efforts with national courts, has proven difficult to implement consistently. Many states, citing concerns about national sovereignty, have either refused to cooperate fully with the ICC's investigations or have actively resisted its jurisdiction. Moreover, the uneven application of justice and the perception of bias in some cases have led to criticisms and calls for reform. Successfully navigating these challenges requires a nuanced understanding of the evolving interplay between state sovereignty and the pursuit of international justice.

Furthermore, the concept of universal jurisdiction, which allows states to prosecute individuals for international crimes regardless of where the crime took place or the nationality of the perpetrator, further complicates the issue. While seemingly a tool to hold perpetrators accountable even where state cooperation is lacking, universal jurisdiction can easily be perceived as an affront to state sovereignty. This tension has been at the heart of numerous diplomatic disputes, underscoring the inherent difficulty in balancing the demands of national sovereignty with the need for international accountability. The absence of clearly defined rules and guidelines around the application of universal jurisdiction further exacerbates this tension. The lack of concrete guidelines makes the implementation of this concept fraught with potential for disagreements and conflicts.

Looking ahead, a constructive solution requires a shift in perspective. Instead of framing the relationship between state sovereignty and international criminal justice as a zero-sum game, we must recognize their interdependent and sometimes complementary nature. The preservation of state sovereignty doesn't necessitate the complete abandonment of international justice mechanisms. Strengthening the ICC through improved cooperation, enhanced judicial efficiency, and a more rigorous adherence to due process can help mitigate concerns about its legitimacy. Simultaneously, states must engage proactively in international dialogue to clarify the limits and applications of universal jurisdiction and mechanisms for collaboration between national and international courts. Striking a balance requires a commitment to both international justice and respect for national sovereignty, a goal that demands ongoing international cooperation and political will. Only through a comprehensive and mutually acceptable framework can we ensure that international crimes are effectively prosecuted while upholding the essential principles of state sovereignty within a rules-based international order. The future of international criminal justice hinges on this delicate balance.

1.2 The Rise of International Justice

The rise of international justice represents a fundamental shift in the global order. For centuries, state sovereignty reigned supreme, a principle shielding states from external interference in their internal affairs. However, the horrors of the 20th century, particularly the systematic atrocities of the World Wars and subsequent genocides, exposed the catastrophic consequences of unchecked state power. The sheer scale of suffering, the deliberate targeting of civilians, and the utter disregard for fundamental human rights demanded a response beyond the capacity of individual states to provide. This imperative, rooted in a shared understanding of humanity's moral failings, spurred the creation of international legal mechanisms designed to hold individuals accountable for crimes against humanity, war crimes, and genocide, irrespective of their nationality or the location of the crime. This marked a profound challenge to the traditional notion of absolute state sovereignty.

This new era of accountability wasn't simply a reaction to past atrocities; it represented a growing recognition of interconnectedness and shared responsibility. The international community, albeit gradually and imperfectly, acknowledged that certain crimes are so heinous they transcend national boundaries, demanding universal condemnation and prosecution. This shift wasn't solely driven by moral outrage; pragmatic considerations also played a critical role. Preventing future atrocities, fostering peace and reconciliation, and promoting the rule of law globally became intertwined with the pursuit of international justice. Ultimately, it became increasingly clear that allowing perpetrators of mass violence to evade justice undermines international stability and perpetuates cycles of conflict.

The establishment of the International Criminal Court (ICC) in 1998 symbolized this transition. The ICC, a permanent international court with jurisdiction to prosecute individuals for the most serious international crimes, represents a significant step toward a global system of justice. However, its development and operation have not been without challenges. The principle of complementarity, designed to balance the ICC's jurisdiction with national justice systems, often results in complex and protracted legal processes. The cooperation of states remains essential to the Court's success, but reluctance by some nations to surrender their citizens or share information highlights the enduring tension between national sovereignty and international justice.

The ICC's work demonstrates both the possibilities and limitations of international criminal justice. While successful prosecutions have provided some measure of justice to victims and their families, they also highlight the immense difficulties involved. The scale of the task - investigating, prosecuting, and ensuring the conviction of perpetrators of large-scale violence - requires significant resources, political will, and enduring international cooperation. The effectiveness of international courts depends not only on their judicial functions but also on the broader political context, encompassing the willingness of states to cooperate and the capacity of the international community to address root causes of conflict. Moreover, achieving real reconciliation often demands more than mere punishment; it necessitates addressing deeper societal issues, including historical grievances and systemic inequalities.

The path towards a more robust and effective system of international criminal justice is far from complete. Navigating the complexities of state sovereignty requires a delicate balance between respecting national interests and upholding fundamental human rights. Furthermore, ensuring the fair and impartial administration of justice for all, regardless of political power or influence, requires continuous vigilance and reform. Yet the pursuit of international justice, though imperfect and frequently challenged, remains a crucial element in the creation of a more peaceful, equitable, and just world order. The journey is ongoing, requiring persistent commitment and cooperation to reconcile the sometimes-conflicting aspirations of state sovereignty and global justice. It demands ongoing dialogues, pragmatic solutions, and a sustained commitment to hold individuals accountable for the gravest crimes against humanity, thereby helping to prevent future atrocities and promoting a more peaceful global environment. The work remains unfinished, but the pursuit of justice continues.

2 Historical Context: Sovereignty's Evolution

The Peace of Westphalia, signed in 1648, is often cited as the birth of the modern state system. This treaty, ending the Thirty Years' War, enshrined the principle of state sovereignty—the absolute authority of a state within its own territory, free from external interference. However, this seemingly absolute power was never truly absolute. Even then, limitations existed, implicitly acknowledged in the very act of negotiating international treaties. The system, while establishing a framework for coexistence, lacked mechanisms to address crimes that transcended national borders. Individual states retained ultimate control over their internal affairs, including the prosecution (or lack thereof) of heinous crimes. This inherent limitation became increasingly apparent as global interconnectedness grew.

Early instances of international cooperation aimed at addressing transnational criminal activities were limited and largely ad hoc. The rise of international law, though initially slow and often contested, started to chip away at the absolute nature of state sovereignty. Early treaties addressing piracy and slavery represent nascent attempts to establish norms exceeding the confines of individual state jurisdiction. These agreements, while significant, operated within a largely state-centric framework, relying on the cooperation of individual nations—cooperation that wasn't always forthcoming. The inherent weakness lay in the absence of a robust enforcement mechanism independent of the sovereign states involved.

The horrors of World War II served as a watershed moment. The sheer scale of atrocities committed during the Holocaust and other wartime crimes exposed the inadequacy of existing international legal structures to address such widespread and systematic violations of human rights. The Nuremberg and Tokyo trials, although controversial regarding their legal basis at the time, demonstrated a willingness to assert jurisdiction over individuals based on the commission of international crimes, even when those crimes occurred within the territory of a sovereign state. This marked a fundamental shift, challenging the absolute supremacy of state sovereignty in the face of grave human rights abuses. The establishment of the United Nations, with its emphasis on international cooperation and human rights, further solidified this evolving perspective.

The post-World War II era witnessed a significant expansion of international law, with numerous conventions and treaties addressing various aspects of international criminal justice. The creation of the International Criminal Court (ICC) in 1998 represents the culmination of this historical evolution. The ICC's establishment marked a momentous step toward creating a truly international system for holding individuals accountable for the most serious crimes of international concern. However, the ICC's existence continues to be fraught with challenges. The principle of complementarity—which allows the ICC to intervene only when national courts are unwilling or unable to prosecute—represents a delicate balance between respecting state sovereignty and ensuring accountability. Many states have been reluctant to cooperate fully with the ICC, highlighting the ongoing tension between national interests and international justice. The differing approaches of states towards the court also indicate that the evolution of international criminal justice is far from over, with constant negotiations and modifications still required.

The very concept of universal jurisdiction, which allows national courts to prosecute individuals for certain international crimes regardless of where the crime occurred or the nationality of the perpetrator or victim, exemplifies the continuing challenge to state sovereignty. While this principle affirms the international community's responsibility to hold perpetrators accountable, it frequently clashes with states' assertions of their exclusive jurisdiction over their territory and citizens. The exercise of universal jurisdiction, in practice, is often met with political resistance and legal challenges, as states seek to protect their perceived national interests. Therefore, navigating the delicate balance between universal jurisdiction and state sovereignty demands careful diplomatic and legal considerations.

Numerous cases demonstrate the practical complexities and compromises involved in achieving international criminal justice. The International Criminal Tribunal for Rwanda (ICTR) and the International Criminal Tribunal for the former Yugoslavia (ICTY), while achieving significant results, also reveal the limitations and challenges of prosecuting large-scale atrocities in post-conflict environments. These tribunals, while groundbreaking, faced substantial challenges in securing cooperation from states, gathering evidence, and navigating complex political landscapes. The ongoing struggle to balance justice with sovereignty remains central to these endeavors, continually redefining the parameters of international law. It highlights the long and difficult road ahead, as well as the constant adaptations needed to face the realities of today.

Therefore, the evolution of sovereignty is a continuous process, an ongoing negotiation between national interests and the collective responsibility to address egregious crimes that violate the fundamental principles of humanity. The future of international criminal justice hinges on finding sustainable solutions that respect state sovereignty while effectively ensuring accountability for serious crimes. This balance demands continued dialogue, cooperation, and a commitment to upholding both national and international norms. Only through this collaborative effort can we hope to achieve a world where justice prevails and the sanctity of human life is upheld.

2.1 Westphalian System and its limits

The Peace of Westphalia, signed in 1648, is often cited as the birth certificate of the modern state system. It enshrined the principle of state sovereignty, granting states exclusive authority within their defined territories. This arrangement, however, wasn't a utopian vision of perfect order; it was a pragmatic compromise forged in the crucible of religious wars, aiming primarily to prevent further large-scale conflicts. Implicit within this system was a significant limitation: the complete absence of any supranational authority capable of enforcing international law or holding states accountable for egregious violations of human rights within their borders.

This inherent flaw became painfully apparent over subsequent centuries. While international law gradually developed, its effectiveness remained profoundly limited by the unwillingness of states to surrender any portion of their hard-won sovereignty. International treaties often lacked robust enforcement mechanisms, rendering them little more than aspirational documents. States were, and largely remain, the primary interpreters and enforcers of international norms, a reality that frequently resulted in a prioritization of national interests over universal justice.

The relative powerlessness of the international community to address atrocities like the Armenian genocide during the First World War, or the numerous instances of mass violence and oppression throughout the 20th century, starkly illustrates the limitations of the Westphalian system. The inherent bias towards state sovereignty consistently hampered efforts to achieve accountability for these crimes. International efforts were often hampered by political maneuvering, national self-interest, and a pervasive lack of willingness to interfere in the internal affairs of other states, even when those affairs involved widespread human rights abuses.

The consequences of this unchecked state sovereignty were, and continue to be, devastating. Mass atrocities, genocide, and crimes against humanity have inflicted immeasurable suffering on countless victims. The very notion of a world where states are free to act with impunity, unconstrained by external checks on their power, is deeply problematic, particularly when viewed through the lens of contemporary human rights norms. These norms—developed largely in response to the horrors of the 20th century—represent a fundamental challenge to the traditional Westphalian conception of absolute state authority.

The development of international criminal law, culminating in the establishment of the International Criminal Court (ICC), represents a significant, albeit imperfect, attempt to overcome these inherent limitations. The ICC's jurisdiction, however, is still heavily circumscribed by state consent and cooperation, reflecting the ongoing struggle between the ideal of universal justice and the reality of national sovereignty. This delicate balance continues to be tested, with various states frequently challenging the Court's authority and jurisdiction, often on the grounds of protecting national interests or asserting sovereignty.

Moreover, the effectiveness of the ICC is constantly hampered by practical challenges. Securing the cooperation of states in apprehending and extraditing suspects remains a persistent obstacle. Many states, particularly those with powerful military or political influence, frequently exhibit reluctance to subject themselves to international scrutiny or to cooperate with ICC investigations, effectively shielding themselves from accountability. This raises complex questions about the viability of truly universal justice within a system still deeply rooted in the principles of Westphalia.

The Westphalian system, while providing a framework for relative stability and preventing some conflicts, has demonstrably failed to adequately address issues of human rights and accountability for serious international crimes. The system's inherent bias towards state sovereignty created a significant gap between the ideal of a just international order and the grim reality of unpunished atrocities. The ongoing evolution of international law and the establishment of international criminal justice mechanisms represent important attempts to rectify this imbalance. However, the tension between state sovereignty and universal justice continues to define the landscape of international relations. The future of international criminal justice depends crucially on the ability to find a sustainable compromise between these two competing principles.

The creation of the ICC and other international tribunals stands as a testament to the growing recognition that the unchecked sovereignty of states is incompatible with the protection of fundamental human rights. However, the ongoing challenges to the

ICC's jurisdiction and effectiveness highlight the deep-seated reluctance of some states to relinquish their absolute power. Successfully navigating this complex terrain requires a delicate balance—respecting state sovereignty while simultaneously ensuring accountability for crimes that shock the conscience of humanity. Only through sustained international cooperation and the evolution of international norms can we hope to create a more just and equitable world order. The legacy of Westphalia continues to resonate, but it is time for a re-evaluation of its principles, one which firmly places human rights at the forefront of international relations. The path forward will undoubtedly require careful consideration of national interests, international law, and the imperative to prevent future atrocities. The goal, however, remains clear: a system that truly balances national sovereignty with the pursuit of universal justice.

2.2 Emergence of International Law

The concept of international law, as a formalized system governing relations between states, didn't spring forth fully formed. Its evolution was a gradual process, shaped by centuries of conflict, cooperation, and shifting power dynamics. Early forms of international regulation existed, primarily through treaties and customary practices among nations, but these lacked the comprehensive structure and enforcement mechanisms we associate with modern international law. These early agreements, often focused on trade, navigation, or specific territorial disputes, were limited in scope and often relied on the goodwill of participating states for compliance. The absence of a central authority to adjudicate disputes or enforce agreements remained a significant obstacle.

The Peace of Westphalia, signed in 1648, is frequently cited as a pivotal moment. While it formalized the state system and principles of sovereignty, it simultaneously revealed inherent limitations in a purely state-centric world. The treaty, while ending a devastating religious war, didn't establish a robust system for preventing future conflicts or addressing international crimes. States retained their primary authority, often prioritizing national interests over broader international norms. This inherent flaw - the lack of supranational authority - would become increasingly apparent over the centuries as international crimes, transcending national boundaries, continued to occur with impunity.

The nineteenth century witnessed the slow but steady growth of international law, driven by advancements in communication and the increasing interdependence of nations. The establishment of international organizations, however rudimentary, such as the International Postal Union, signaled a growing recognition of the need for cooperation beyond bilateral agreements. The codification of certain customary norms into treaties, such as those relating to the laws of war, further contributed to the development of a more formal legal framework. However, the enforcement of these rules remained largely dependent on the willingness of states to cooperate, creating significant limitations in practice.

The horrors of the two World Wars provided a catalyst for a paradigm shift in international relations. The sheer scale of atrocities committed during these conflicts, including widespread genocide and crimes against humanity, exposed the inadequacy of existing international mechanisms in preventing and punishing such violations. The world community increasingly recognized the need for a stronger international legal framework to address such crimes, recognizing that individual accountability, rather than just state responsibility, was critical. This recognition laid the groundwork for the creation of the Nuremberg and Tokyo Tribunals, marking a significant departure from previous approaches and setting a precedent for the prosecution of individuals for international crimes.

Post-World War II witnessed a surge in activity aimed at strengthening international law. The establishment of the United Nations, with its Charter emphasizing international cooperation and the prevention of future wars, reflected this global shift. The creation of various specialized agencies, focusing on specific areas such as human rights, refugee protection, and international criminal justice, further solidified the development of a more integrated and sophisticated international legal system. The subsequent establishment of the International Criminal Court in 1998 represented the culmination of decades of efforts to create a permanent institution for the prosecution of the most serious international crimes. Its creation signifies a crucial step towards a system where individual accountability is paramount, even when national sovereignty might be implicated. However, the path ahead remains complex, fraught with challenges as the world seeks to balance the principles of state sovereignty with the urgent need for international justice. The ICC's success hinges on sustained international cooperation, political will, and ongoing efforts to address its inherent limitations. The journey towards a fully effective international legal order, capable of preventing and punishing serious crimes, is a continuous process of refinement, adaptation and engagement with the evolving challenges of global governance. It is a testament to humanity's constant struggle to reconcile its inherent need for order and justice with the complex realities of sovereign states.

2.3 Post-WWII Developments

The aftermath of World War II witnessed a profound shift in the global landscape, irrevocably altering the traditional understanding of state sovereignty. The horrors of the Holocaust and other atrocities committed during the war exposed the inadequacies of the existing international legal framework in preventing and punishing such crimes. This stark reality fueled a growing international consensus that states could no longer claim absolute sovereignty as a shield against accountability for egregious violations of human rights and international law. The Nuremberg and Tokyo trials, although controversial in their application of ex post facto law, established a critical precedent, demonstrating the international community's willingness to assert jurisdiction over individuals for crimes against humanity, war crimes, and crimes against peace. These trials, while imperfect, laid the foundation for future international criminal justice mechanisms.

The creation of the United Nations in 1945 marked another pivotal moment. The UN Charter, while upholding the principle of state sovereignty, simultaneously recognized the need for international cooperation to maintain international peace and security. This inherent tension between state sovereignty and international cooperation became a central theme in the development of international criminal justice. The UN's role in establishing ad hoc tribunals for the former Yugoslavia and Rwanda further solidified this trend, demonstrating a willingness to intervene in situations where national judicial systems were unable or unwilling to prosecute serious international crimes. These tribunals, though facing various challenges, successfully prosecuted numerous high-ranking officials, solidifying the principle that individuals could be held accountable for their actions even when those actions were committed under the auspices of a state.

Moreover, the post-war era saw the burgeoning of international human rights law. The Universal Declaration of Human Rights, adopted in 1948, enshrined fundamental human rights and freedoms, placing limitations on state sovereignty. This development, while initially aspirational, progressively gained traction, leading to the adoption of numerous international human rights treaties. These treaties, while not directly addressing criminal accountability, nevertheless underscored the evolving understanding of state obligations towards its citizens and the broader international community. The increasing recognition of human rights norms influenced the development of international criminal law, shifting the focus from a purely state-centric approach towards one that prioritized individual rights and accountability.

The Cold War period, while marked by geopolitical tensions, did not completely halt the momentum of international criminal justice. The emergence of international humanitarian law continued, particularly through the development of the Geneva Conventions and their Protocols. This evolution of law aimed to protect civilians and other non-combatants during armed conflicts and limited the permissible actions of states in times of war. This body of law, while focused on the conduct of warfare, further emphasized limitations on state sovereignty in the pursuit of preserving human dignity. The gradual expansion of international humanitarian law, alongside the increasing acceptance of international human rights standards, served to lay the groundwork for the creation of the International Criminal Court (ICC).

The establishment of the ICC in 1998 marked a significant milestone, representing a formal and permanent international judicial mechanism for prosecuting individuals for serious international crimes. Although the ICC's jurisdiction is not universal and its operation has faced various challenges, its very existence symbolized a decisive shift in the global balance between state sovereignty and international justice. The court's ability to exert pressure on states to cooperate in investigations and prosecutions, alongside its potential to hold individuals accountable for their actions regardless of nationality or the state in which they committed crimes, represents a profound departure from the traditional Westphalian system. The challenges faced by the ICC, ranging from issues of state cooperation to concerns about selectivity and bias, underscore the ongoing tensions between the pursuit of international justice and the preservation of state sovereignty. Yet, these challenges do not diminish the fundamental significance of the ICC as a powerful symbol of the evolving international legal order and the growing limitations on absolute state sovereignty.

3 International Criminal Court: Jurisdiction and Challenges

The International Criminal Court (ICC), established in 2002, represents a significant, albeit imperfect, step towards achieving international criminal justice. Its mandate centers on prosecuting individuals for the gravest crimes of international concern: genocide, war crimes, crimes against humanity, and the crime of aggression. This jurisdiction, however, is not unlimited. The Rome Statute, the ICC's founding document, meticulously outlines the court's powers and limitations, aiming to strike a balance between international justice and the principle of state sovereignty. Critically, the ICC isn't meant to supplant national legal systems; instead, it operates under the principle of complementarity.

This complementarity principle is fundamental to the ICC's operation. It dictates that the Court should only exercise its jurisdiction when national courts are unwilling or unable genuinely to investigate or prosecute crimes falling within the Court's competence. This carefully constructed framework attempts to respect state sovereignty by allowing national justice systems the primary role in pursuing accountability. However, determining whether a state's legal system is genuinely unwilling or unable to act remains a significant challenge, often involving complex political and legal assessments. The Court's decisions in this regard are frequently scrutinized and debated.

State cooperation is undeniably crucial to the ICC's success. The Court relies heavily on states to arrest suspects, surrender them to The Hague, and provide evidence. Yet, the reality is frequently far from ideal. Many states, particularly those with strong national interests at stake, are reluctant to cooperate fully, citing concerns about sovereignty or political considerations. This lack of consistent cooperation significantly hampers the Court's effectiveness, forcing it to rely on a limited range of tools and strategies for securing its objectives. The resulting jurisdictional gaps and enforcement limitations severely constrain the impact of the ICC's actions.

The ICC has faced considerable criticism since its inception. Some accuse it of bias, focusing disproportionately on African states while ignoring alleged atrocities in powerful nations. This perception, whether accurate or not, significantly damages the Court's credibility and undermines its legitimacy in the eyes of many. Other critiques target its lengthy and complex procedures, which can lead to prolonged trials and the perception of injustice being slow to arrive. There have been calls for significant reforms to address these criticisms, including enhancing the

Court's transparency and improving its efficiency. These calls reflect the ongoing tensions between the ambitious aims of international criminal justice and the realities of international relations. Assessing the ICC's effectiveness remains a complex undertaking. While it has secured several convictions, its impact on preventing future atrocities and promoting international justice is a subject of ongoing debate. The Court's successes are often overshadowed by the challenges it faces in securing cooperation and navigating the complex political landscape. Ultimately, judging its effectiveness requires a nuanced approach, considering not only the number of convictions, but also its influence on national justice systems, the deterrence effect of its existence, and its contribution to the evolution of international law. While some argue that it has already made a positive impact, improving its effectiveness requires continuous reflection, adaptation, and improvement. Ultimately, its influence will depend on increased international cooperation and a willingness to balance state sovereignty with the pursuit of justice. The court's future trajectory will largely depend on the political will of individual states to support and empower it.

3.1 The ICC's Mandate

The International Criminal Court (ICC), established in 2002 under the Rome Statute, possesses a mandate significantly impacting state sovereignty. Its primary function is to investigate and prosecute individuals accused of the gravest crimes of concern to the international community: genocide, crimes against humanity, war crimes, and the crime of aggression. This mandate, however, is not absolute; it operates within a carefully constructed framework designed to balance the pursuit of international justice with the principle of state sovereignty.

The Rome Statute meticulously defines the Court's jurisdiction, emphasizing the principle of complementarity. This principle dictates that the ICC only exercises its jurisdiction when national courts are unwilling or unable genuinely to investigate or prosecute such crimes. It prevents the ICC from overriding national judicial systems unnecessarily, respecting state sovereignty in the first instance. However, the Court's jurisdiction also extends to situations referred by the UN Security Council, irrespective of the state's willingness to cooperate, highlighting the potential for limitations on national sovereignty in certain circumstances. The delicate balance between these jurisdictional provisions is frequently tested, presenting ongoing challenges to the Court's operation.

Critically, the ICC's mandate relies heavily on the cooperation of states. The Statute requires states to cooperate with the Court in various ways, including surrendering suspects, providing evidence, and enforcing sentences. However, cooperation levels vary significantly. Some states are enthusiastic supporters, actively assisting the Court's investigations and prosecutions. Others, however, are reluctant or openly hostile, citing concerns about national sovereignty and their own domestic legal systems. This lack of universal cooperation remains a significant obstacle to the effective exercise of the ICC's mandate, creating jurisdictional gaps and hindering justice.

The ICC's mandate has faced numerous criticisms since its inception. Some states argue that the Court is biased against certain countries or regions, leading to accusations of neo-colonialism. Others criticize its perceived inefficiency and its high costs, questioning its overall effectiveness. Still others express concern about the Court's potential to intrude upon the internal affairs of sovereign states, potentially undermining national security interests or jeopardizing delicate peace processes. These criticisms highlight the deeply complex and often politically charged nature of the ICC's mandate and its implications for international relations.

To address such criticisms and strengthen its effectiveness, several reforms have been proposed. These include enhancing the Court's capacity to conduct investigations and prosecutions more efficiently and cost-effectively, improving its outreach and communication strategies to foster better understanding and cooperation, and further clarifying the application of the complementarity principle to avoid jurisdictional overlaps or conflicts. Discussions also focus on addressing concerns about representation and ensuring the Court's impartiality. These reforms aim to strengthen the ICC's mandate, improve its legitimacy, and enhance its effectiveness in delivering justice while respecting state sovereignty. The ongoing debate reflects the continued struggle to reconcile these potentially conflicting goals. Reform efforts are crucial to navigating the ongoing challenges and strengthen-

ing the Court's impact on international criminal justice.
The ICC's mandate therefore represents a complex interplay between the pursuit of international justice and the preservation of state sovereignty. It's a dynamic and evolving mechanism, constantly adapting to both successes and challenges. Its ongoing effectiveness hinges on a continuous balancing act between international accountability and respect for national jurisdictions, a process requiring constant negotiation and reform to strengthen international cooperation and ensure fairness in the pursuit of justice for victims of egregious crimes. The future of the ICC's mandate rests on the international community's capacity to navigate these complexities and find sustainable solutions to ensure justice prevails without compromising the legitimacy and essential role of national legal systems. Only through careful consideration and decisive action can we strive towards a system where both international justice and national sovereignty are effectively protected and nurtured. The implications are far-reaching and require continuous attention from policymakers, legal scholars, and the international community as a whole.

3.2 Complementarity Principle

The Rome Statute's Complementarity Principle is a cornerstone of the International Criminal Court (ICC), designed to prevent the Court from overshadowing national judicial systems. It operates on the premise that national courts should be the primary avenue for prosecuting international crimes. The ICC steps in only when a state is unwilling or unable genuinely to investigate or prosecute such crimes itself. This principle, therefore, hinges on a delicate balance - ensuring accountability for heinous acts while respecting state sovereignty. Its success relies not only on the ICC's effectiveness but crucially on the willingness and capacity of states to fulfill their primary prosecutorial role. Understanding this complex interplay is vital to grasping the ICC's true potential.

The principle's implementation is far from straightforward. Defining "unwillingness" and "inability" requires careful consideration of a state's actions or inactions. A state might genuinely lack the resources or expertise to handle complex international crime investigations, leading to an inability to prosecute. Conversely, a state could actively obstruct investigations or shield perpetrators, demonstrating unwillingness. The ICC's Pre-Trial Chamber plays a critical role in assessing these situations, examining the state's actions through a rigorous lens. This process frequently involves engaging with the national authorities concerned, attempting to encourage cooperation and foster a collaborative approach before initiating an ICC investigation.

Interpreting the principle has led to numerous legal debates and decisions. The ICC's prosecutorial decisions, based on its interpretation of complementarity, have been subject to intense scrutiny, prompting diverse legal analyses. Critics argue that the bar for establishing "unwillingness" is too high, allowing states to evade their responsibilities. Others contend that the ICC's intervention should be more proactive, particularly in situations where national courts are demonstrably biased or compromised. These varying perspectives highlight the persistent challenges in striking the right balance between national sovereignty and international justice. The ongoing discussions and revisions of the ICC's procedures reflect this enduring tension.

The practical application of complementarity frequently involves navigating intricate political considerations. The ICC's investigations can spark diplomatic tensions, especially when involving powerful states or influential individuals. States may view ICC involvement as an infringement on their sovereignty, leading to resistance and non-cooperation. This political dimension complicates the already challenging legal framework, underscoring the delicate balance required. Navigating these complexities demands both legal expertise and acute political sensitivity from both the ICC and individual states. The ICC has had to find creative diplomatic solutions to encourage cooperation while maintaining impartiality.

Moving forward, strengthening the complementarity principle requires a multifaceted approach. Improved communication and capacity-building initiatives are crucial. The ICC can offer technical assistance and training to national judicial systems, fostering improved investigative capabilities and strengthening their capacity to handle international crimes. This proactive engagement can improve the chances of national courts meeting the required standards, reducing the need for ICC intervention and promoting genuine complementarity, rather than simply deferring prosecution. Simultaneously, states must actively prioritize investigations into international crimes, demonstrating a clear commitment to justice.

Ultimately, the success of the complementarity principle rests on fostering a genuine partnership between the ICC and national courts. It's not a zero-sum game; rather, it's a cooperative endeavour where both actors contribute to upholding justice and respecting state sovereignty. Open dialogue, mutual respect, and a shared commitment to the rule of law are fundamental to this partnership's success. Only through such collaboration can the ICC effectively fulfill its mandate, ensuring accountability for the gravest crimes while safeguarding the principles of national sovereignty. The delicate balance between these two elements will continue to be at the forefront of discussions in international law and the quest for global justice. The path forward involves a continuous dialogue between states, international institutions, and civil society to refine the mechanisms of complementarity and ensure its effective and fair application.

3.3 State Cooperation & Obstacles

Effective state cooperation is the bedrock of a functional International Criminal Court (ICC). Without it, the ICC's mandate remains largely symbolic, a powerful aspiration hampered by practical realities. Many states, prioritizing national interests and sensitivities, are hesitant to fully cooperate, leading to significant challenges in investigations and prosecutions. This reluctance stems from a variety of factors, often intertwining legal and political considerations.

National sovereignty concerns often dominate the debate. Some states view ICC investigations as an infringement upon their internal affairs, a violation of their right to self-determination. The perception of external interference in domestic judicial processes can be particularly acute in states with fragile political systems or historical sensitivities surrounding national identity. This perception is not always unfounded; the ICC's actions, if not carefully managed, can indeed undermine state authority and create further political instability.

Legal obstacles further complicate matters. Many states lack the legal frameworks or resources to fully comply with ICC requests for evidence, witness testimony, or the arrest and transfer of suspects. Differences in legal systems and definitions of crimes can also create significant roadblocks. Even with the best intentions, navigating complex legal procedures across multiple jurisdictions presents a considerable logistical hurdle. This often translates into delays, missed opportunities, and ultimately, a weakened capacity for international justice.

Political calculations are never far from the surface. States may choose to withhold cooperation based on their strategic relationships with other nations, especially if suspects hold positions of power or influence within those states. These political dynamics can create powerful incentives to shield individuals from international justice, regardless of the gravity of their alleged crimes. Furthermore, a reluctance to set precedents that might expose their own officials to future prosecution often fuels non-cooperation.

The effects of insufficient state cooperation are far-reaching. It weakens the ICC's ability to deter future atrocities and to hold perpetrators accountable for past crimes. This undermines the very purpose of the Court—to ensure that egregious violations of international law do not go unpunished. In essence, the lack of cooperation represents a significant failure of the international community to create a truly effective system of international criminal justice. Justice delayed is justice denied, and the obstacles to state cooperation actively contribute to that delay.

Addressing these challenges requires a multi-pronged approach. Strengthening international legal frameworks to clearly define obligations and responsibilities can improve compliance. Providing technical assistance and capacity building to states to help them meet their obligations is equally crucial. This might involve training legal professionals, improving investigative capabilities, and providing resources to update national legislation. Promoting a better understanding of the ICC's mandate and its role in upholding international justice is essential to alleviate fears of interference. Open dialogue and diplomacy can go a long way toward building trust and fostering cooperation.

Ultimately, achieving a greater level of state cooperation is vital for the long-term success of the ICC. This requires not only addressing the practical and legal challenges but also engaging with the political realities that shape state behavior. It is a continuous process that demands sustained commitment from the international community, as well as a recognition of the intricate balance between national sovereignty and the imperative of international justice. Effective mechanisms for conflict resolution and dispute settlement can contribute significantly to overcoming these obstacles. The goal, however, remains the same: ensuring accountability for those who commit the most heinous crimes, while carefully respecting the sovereignty of states. This requires consistent effort and sustained dialogue to find the delicate equilibrium between the two. Therefore, fostering mutual understanding and respect must be the primary focus of any strategic approach.

3.4 Criticisms and Reforms

The International Criminal Court (ICC), despite its laudable objectives, faces persistent criticism. Some states, particularly powerful ones, perceive its actions as an infringement on their national sovereignty, arguing that the Court oversteps its mandate by prosecuting individuals from countries unwilling to cooperate. This perception fuels a reluctance to fully engage with the ICC's processes, hindering its effectiveness in bringing perpetrators of heinous crimes to justice. Furthermore, the principle of complementarity, while intended to respect national judicial systems, has proven problematic in practice. Many states lack the capacity or the will to prosecute these crimes effectively, leaving a significant gap in accountability that the ICC struggles to fill. The sheer complexity of navigating legal systems across different jurisdictions adds another layer of difficulty, causing delays and frustrations. This further intensifies the criticism surrounding the ICC's functionality and effectiveness.

The criticisms extend beyond sovereignty concerns. Resource constraints significantly limit the ICC's operational capacity. Investigations and prosecutions are incredibly resource-intensive, necessitating considerable funding and skilled personnel. The imbalance of resources available to the ICC and those available to powerful states defending against ICC prosecutions creates a significant disparity that threatens fairness. This uneven playing field is a major cause for concern, and it fuels criticisms about the lack of genuine equality before the law. The lack of universal ratification and the resulting patchy jurisdictional reach is also a major drawback.

Several reform proposals aim to address these criticisms. Strengthening the ICC's budget and staffing levels is crucial. This would enhance its investigative and prosecutorial capabilities, enabling a more efficient and thorough approach to cases. Improved cooperation mechanisms with states are essential to facilitate the arrest and transfer of suspects. Incentivizing cooperation, rather than relying solely on pressure, might involve offering technical assistance to states lacking the necessary resources or expertise to conduct their own investigations. Transparency in the court's processes could address concerns about bias and ensure greater legitimacy. Increased dialogue with states that are hesitant to engage with the Court is also paramount, aiming to address their concerns and build trust.

Furthermore, exploring alternative dispute resolution mechanisms could offer a way to manage conflicts without resorting to full-scale prosecutions. These alternative mechanisms could be employed in situations where national jurisdictions are willing and capable but require support to conduct effective investigations and trials. The goal here is to create a system that is more flexible and adaptable, better responding to the varying capacities and political realities of different states. The potential for creating specialized chambers within the ICC focusing on specific crimes or geographic regions is also an area of discussion. This could improve efficiency and allow a deeper level of expertise and focus on particular types of international crimes that require unique skills and knowledge. This could lead to swifter and more effective justice.

Ultimately, reforming the ICC requires a multifaceted approach. It necessitates bolstering the Court's resources, enhancing its cooperation mechanisms with states, increasing transparency in its operations, and promoting dialogue to build trust and understanding. This combined strategy is crucial to navigate the challenges posed by state sovereignty while simultaneously ensuring accountability for the gravest crimes under international law. Success hinges on fostering a culture of collaboration between the ICC and national judicial systems, recognizing that both play a critical role in upholding justice on a global scale. This careful balancing act requires persistent diplomacy and a strong commitment from all stakeholders to effectively reconcile the often-competing demands of state sovereignty and international criminal justice. The path ahead is not easy, yet the pursuit of justice necessitates overcoming the substantial challenges that lie ahead. Only then can a more effective and just international criminal justice system be realized. The road to reform is complex, demanding a collective and sustained effort from the international community.

3.5 Effectiveness Evaluation

Assessing the International Criminal Court's (ICC) effectiveness requires a multifaceted approach, moving beyond simple conviction rates. We must consider the ICC's impact on national legal systems, its deterrent effect on potential perpetrators, and its contribution to broader peacebuilding efforts. While the ICC has secured convictions, its influence extends far beyond individual prosecutions. The very existence of the Court has prompted states to strengthen their own domestic mechanisms for prosecuting international crimes, a significant step towards holding perpetrators accountable at a national level. This ripple effect, a crucial but often overlooked aspect of the ICC's influence, should be central to any genuine evaluation of its impact.

The ICC's influence on national legal reforms is demonstrably substantial. Numerous countries have amended their domestic laws to criminalize acts previously unaddressed, spurred on by the ICC's focus on specific crimes against humanity and war crimes. Furthermore, the Court has catalysed the development of national capacities for investigation and prosecution, providing training and technical assistance to states facing resource constraints. This capacity-building, a form of indirect impact, is arguably as important as the direct prosecutions themselves, leading to a significant enhancement of the global response to serious international crimes.

However, the ICC's effectiveness is not without its critics. Some argue that the Court's focus on high-profile individuals overshadows the need for addressing systemic issues that contribute to such crimes. Others point to the slow pace of investigations and prosecutions, the complex interplay with national jurisdictions, and the limitations imposed by state cooperation, raising concerns about the Court's real-world influence. Yet even these criticisms highlight the Court's engagement with complex real-world issues. The challenges faced in securing cooperation from states, or the complexities of navigating complementary jurisdictions, are direct reflections of the difficult power dynamics at play in the global arena.

Therefore, a comprehensive evaluation must consider the long-term consequences of the ICC's actions. The Court's deterrent effect is difficult to quantify directly; however, the mere threat of prosecution can influence the behaviour of powerful actors. Similarly, the ICC's role in promoting transitional justice and reconciliation, though often indirect, is significant. By creating a space for victims to voice their experiences and seek redress, the ICC contributes to a broader process of healing and peacebuilding in post-conflict societies. The long-term impact on national justice systems, post-conflict reconciliation efforts, and international norm-setting are all areas deserving serious consideration.

Ultimately, judging the ICC's effectiveness necessitates a shift from solely focusing on individual convictions to a holistic perspective. The Court's influence extends far beyond the courtroom, impacting national legal frameworks, influencing state behaviour, fostering institutional capacity building, and contributing to international norm development. This broader approach requires careful consideration of the numerous interconnected aspects of the Court's impact, acknowledging the complexities inherent in evaluating its contributions to international justice. A successful evaluation cannot simply tally convictions; it must consider the subtle yet significant influence the Court exerts upon the global legal landscape and the long-term effects of its actions. By recognizing the intricate web of relationships within international law and its practical applications, we can obtain a more informed and useful conclusion on the ICC's impact.

Analyzing the ICC's influence demands moving beyond simplistic metrics. A purely quantitative assessment, focusing solely on the number of convictions, neglects the significant qualitative effects on national legal systems, peacebuilding processes, and the shaping of international norms. The ICC's capacity building initiatives, its subtle but influential pressure on state behavior, and its long-term contribution to transitional justice are crucial aspects which numbers alone cannot adequately capture. The challenge lies in developing robust methodologies that can effectively assess these nuanced and intangible aspects of the ICC's contributions.

The assessment should also address the inherent limitations faced by the ICC. Political considerations, resource constraints, and the complexities of international cooperation invariably constrain the Court's capabilities. Acknowledging these factors is not an excuse for inaction; rather, it necessitates a nuanced and realistic understanding of the challenges and limitations the ICC faces in fulfilling its mandate. Only with such an understanding can future strategies for strengthening the Court be developed effectively. The interaction between the court and state sovereignty, while fraught with tension, is also vital in assessing its full effectiveness. A genuine assessment needs to balance these conflicting forces and incorporate this crucial element of the international justice system.

Furthermore, comparative analysis with other international criminal tribunals and national prosecutions can help in accurately evaluating the ICC's effectiveness. By comparing outcomes, methodologies, and challenges, we can glean valuable insights into best practices and identify areas for improvement. This comparative approach necessitates an understanding of various legal and political systems, emphasizing the inherent complexities associated with enforcing international justice. This requires a truly interdisciplinary understanding of law, political science, sociology and other crucial related areas of study, in order to contextualize the data.

Therefore, a comprehensive evaluation of the ICC's effectiveness requires a multi-faceted approach. It should account for the court's direct impact through convictions, its indirect influence on state legislation and capacity building, the long-term consequences on peace and reconciliation, and the significant impact it has had in establishing international norms related to accountability for international crimes. Further, this must take into account the limitations inherent in the international legal framework, the interplay of state sovereignty and the court's jurisdiction, and the long and complex processes of international justice. This holistic approach to evaluating the ICC offers a clearer understanding of its true value and impact on the international legal landscape.

4 National Sovereignty vs. Universal Jurisdiction

Universal jurisdiction, a principle allowing states to prosecute individuals for egregious international crimes irrespective of the crime's location or the perpetrator's nationality, presents a complex challenge to traditional notions of state sovereignty. This principle, rooted in the idea of universal human rights violations demanding international redress, directly conflicts with the long-standing principle of state sovereignty, which asserts a nation's absolute authority within its borders. The tension stems from the potential infringement upon a state's exclusive right to exercise jurisdiction over individuals within its territory, potentially leading to diplomatic friction and strained international relations. This is particularly relevant given the increasing interconnectedness of the global community.

The assertion of universal jurisdiction often involves complex legal and political considerations. For instance, a state might choose to prosecute an individual for crimes against humanity committed elsewhere, even if that individual holds no connection to that state, beyond the severity of the crimes. This action directly challenges the principle of territorial jurisdiction and can be viewed as an overreach by other nations. The decision to exercise universal jurisdiction reflects a state's commitment to international justice, but it also raises questions about its legitimacy and the potential for abuse. The absence of clear universally accepted guidelines further complicates matters. What constitutes sufficient evidence? How can potential biases be avoided? These are critical questions that need careful consideration to ensure fairness and prevent misapplication.

Several cases have underscored the contentious relationship between universal jurisdiction and national sovereignty. Spain's attempts to prosecute former Chilean dictator Augusto Pinochet for human rights abuses, though ultimately unsuccessful in its initial form, sparked intense debate about the limits of universal jurisdiction and the potential for politically motivated prosecutions. Similarly, the prosecutions of individuals involved in the Rwandan genocide, though largely successful in bringing perpetrators to justice, still raised concerns among some states regarding interference with their internal affairs. These situations highlight the difficulties inherent in balancing the need to hold perpetrators of serious international crimes accountable with the principles of state sovereignty and non-interference. This delicate balance requires careful diplomatic navigation and robust international cooperation.

The conflict is further exacerbated by the lack of a universally agreed-upon definition of universal jurisdiction and the absence of a clear enforcement mechanism. This ambiguity allows states to interpret and apply the principle in vastly different ways, leading to inconsistencies and potential for arbitrary action. The challenge lies in finding a practical framework that respects the principle of state sovereignty while simultaneously ensuring accountability for serious crimes that transcend national borders and violate fundamental human rights. Without a robust, universally accepted framework, the exercise of universal jurisdiction risks becoming a tool for political maneuvering, undermining its intended purpose and further straining international relations.

One possible approach to mitigating the conflict is through enhanced international cooperation. This involves states actively engaging in discussions to develop clearer guidelines and standards for the exercise of universal jurisdiction, focusing on situations where the principle is most critically needed, and avoiding its use in a manner that is politically motivated. Furthermore, improved communication and information sharing amongst states could help reduce instances of conflicting claims of jurisdiction and create a system that is perceived as fairer and more equitable. Robust mechanisms for dispute resolution could also minimize friction. Ultimately, any effective strategy requires a willingness to compromise and a recognition that balancing sovereignty with the pursuit of justice is an ongoing process, requiring continuous dialogue and refinement.

Ultimately, navigating the complexities of national sovereignty and universal jurisdiction requires a nuanced understanding of the interplay between these competing principles. The challenge isn't in discarding one in favor of the other, but rather in establishing a framework that allows for the effective prosecution of perpetrators of serious international crimes while simultaneously respecting the fundamental principle of state sovereignty. This requires a commitment to international cooperation, the development of clear and consistent standards, and a willingness to engage in continuous dialogue and refinement of the existing mechanisms. Only through such collaborative efforts can we hope to achieve a balance that ensures both accountability for heinous crimes and the preservation of national self-determination. The path forward necessitates a multifaceted approach that acknowledges the legitimate concerns of states while safeguarding the principles of international justice and the universal human rights they seek to protect. The challenge is not to choose between sovereignty and justice but to forge a path where both can coexist and flourish.

4.1 Defining Universal Jurisdiction

Universal jurisdiction is a complex legal principle that asserts a state's right to prosecute individuals for serious international crimes, regardless of where the crime was committed or the nationality of the perpetrator or victim. This principle stands in contrast to the traditional notion of state sovereignty, which emphasizes a state's exclusive authority within its own territory. The tension between these two concepts is a central theme in discussions about international criminal justice.

Historically, the concept of universal jurisdiction emerged from customary international law and was gradually codified in various treaties and national legislation. It gained prominence following the atrocities of World War II, when the international community recognized the need for mechanisms to hold individuals accountable for crimes against humanity, war crimes, and genocide, even if their own states were unwilling or unable to do so. The principle's application, however, is far from straightforward, often sparking intense debate and legal challenges.

One of the main criticisms levelled against universal jurisdiction is that it potentially infringes upon state sovereignty. States argue that it undermines their exclusive right to exercise jurisdiction over individuals within their territory. Concerns also exist regarding the potential for abuse, with accusations of politically motivated prosecutions. However, proponents emphasize that universal jurisdiction serves as a crucial safeguard against impunity for perpetrators of egregious international crimes, ensuring accountability where national justice systems fail.

The application of universal jurisdiction varies considerably across countries. Some states have incorporated it broadly into their domestic legal frameworks, while others have adopted a more restrictive approach, applying it only in specific circumstances or limiting it to certain crimes. The criteria for exercising universal jurisdiction often include the gravity of the crime, the presence of the suspect on the state's territory, and the absence of prosecution by the state where the crime was committed. This last point is particularly important in demonstrating the principle's intention to fill gaps, not to usurp national legal systems. Furthermore, the issue of jurisdiction often involves intricate questions of international law, including principles of state immunity, extradition, and the relationship between national and international courts. The interplay between these factors contributes to the complexities surrounding the practical implementation of universal jurisdiction. Decisions on whether to prosecute individuals under universal jurisdiction often involve careful consideration of several factors, including political implications and potential diplomatic consequences.

Defining the scope of universal jurisdiction is crucial. It's essential to carefully delineate the categories of crimes to which it applies, ensuring that it is not applied arbitrarily or in a manner inconsistent with international law. This necessitates a clear definition of international crimes, as well as well-established standards of evidence and due process to protect the rights of the accused. The lack of a globally unified approach to universal jurisdiction further complicates its implementation.

Many argue that greater clarity and harmonization are needed in international law to regulate and strengthen the application of universal jurisdiction. This includes developing more precise definitions of crimes, enhancing procedures for cooperation between states, and strengthening mechanisms for ensuring fair trials. This would need to occur while also maintaining respect for state sovereignty. This delicate balance is crucial to avoid undermining the effectiveness of universal jurisdiction while respecting states' rights.

The future of universal jurisdiction likely hinges on fostering greater international cooperation and developing clearer legal standards. This requires not only legal frameworks but also political will and commitment from states to ensure that those responsible for egregious international crimes are brought to justice, regardless of where they are located or their nationality. Achieving this balance requires careful consideration, dialogue, and a willingness to compromise on the part of both supporters and critics of universal jurisdiction. The development of robust and consistent legal frameworks within the international system is also vital. The aim should be to create a system that is both effective and respectful of fundamental legal principles.

Successfully navigating the complexities of universal jurisdiction necessitates a nuanced understanding of its origins, its current practical application, and the ongoing challenges to its effective implementation. A collaborative approach, involving states, international organizations, and legal experts, is essential to ensure that universal jurisdiction remains a vital tool for addressing international crimes without compromising state sovereignty or the fundamental rights of individuals. Only through a commitment to international cooperation and a refinement of legal frameworks can the global community effectively address the persistent challenges of impunity for perpetrators of serious crimes. The path forward necessitates a delicate dance between holding individuals accountable for grave offenses and respecting the principles of national sovereignty. Ultimately, the long-term success of universal jurisdiction depends on the ability of the international community to foster a system of justice that upholds both accountability and respect for the rule of law.

4.2 Conflicts and Tensions

The inherent tension between national sovereignty and universal jurisdiction stems from fundamentally different conceptions of authority. State sovereignty, traditionally understood, asserts a state's absolute authority within its borders, free from external interference. Universal jurisdiction, conversely, posits that certain crimes—grave breaches of international humanitarian law, genocide, war crimes—transcend national boundaries, demanding prosecution regardless of where the crime occurred or the perpetrator's nationality. This clash is not merely theoretical; it manifests in real-world conflicts over the prosecution of individuals accused of heinous crimes.

States understandably resist what they perceive as intrusions on their sovereignty. The surrender of a national to an international court can be seen as an affront to national pride and a compromise of the state's capacity to maintain order and dispense justice within its own borders. This feeling is particularly acute in nations with a history of resisting external interference or those where the accused holds a position of power or influence within the state. Such resistance can range from outright refusal to cooperate with international investigations and prosecutions to the enactment of domestic laws designed to limit or prevent the exercise of universal jurisdiction.

Conversely, the advocates for universal jurisdiction argue that the gravity of certain crimes necessitates a mechanism for accountability that surpasses national boundaries. The argument emphasizes the need to prevent impunity for perpetrators of atrocities and to affirm the international community's collective responsibility to protect fundamental human rights. They see universal jurisdiction as a crucial tool in deterring future crimes and ensuring that victims obtain justice even when national justice systems are unwilling or unable to act. This is particularly pertinent when dealing with mass atrocities where national courts may be either overwhelmed or complicit in the crimes themselves.

The practical consequences of this tension are often complex and multifaceted. Diplomatic relations can be strained, leading to political tensions and even boycotts. States may withdraw from international agreements or refuse to ratify treaties that enhance the reach of international criminal justice mechanisms. There have also been instances of states using countermeasures, such as arresting judges or officials from other countries involved in proceedings concerning their nationals. This highlights how deeply the struggle over sovereignty impacts the international legal landscape.

Successfully navigating this complex terrain necessitates a nuanced understanding of the competing interests at play. Simply advocating for one position at the expense of the other is unlikely to yield sustainable solutions. Instead, a more productive approach focuses on finding common ground through mechanisms that balance the legitimate concerns of states with the imperative of bringing perpetrators of atrocity crimes to justice. This might involve strengthening international cooperation, improving communication and the sharing of evidence, and enhancing the capacity of national judicial systems to deal with such cases. It also demands a commitment to the principles of due process and fair trial, ensuring that individuals are not subjected to arbitrary or politically motivated prosecution.

The tension between state sovereignty and universal jurisdiction is a persistent challenge in the evolving field of international criminal justice. There are no easy answers, and the path to a harmonious balance requires continuous dialogue, compromise, and a recognition of the value of both preserving state sovereignty and securing justice for victims of grave international crimes. The future of international criminal justice hinges on our ability to bridge this divide, ensuring accountability without undermining the fundamental principles that underpin international relations. This requires a willingness to engage with the complexities of this challenge, to listen to diverse perspectives, and to approach the matter with the understanding that no one solution satisfies all sides fully. Ultimately, the process will likely involve a gradual shift in the balance of power as the scope of international criminal justice expands, and as states begin to recognize their interconnectedness within the international community. Therefore, the challenge requires thoughtful examination, compromise, and ongoing refinement of international law to adapt to evolving realities.

5 Case Studies: Conflicts and Compromises

The International Criminal Tribunal for Rwanda (ICTR), established in 1994, grappled with the immense challenge of prosecuting those responsible for the Rwandan genocide. Its mandate, to bring to justice perpetrators of serious violations of international humanitarian law, clashed directly with Rwanda's assertion of sovereignty over its own judicial processes. The ICTR's jurisdiction, based on the UN Security Council's resolutions, represented a significant incursion into Rwanda's internal affairs, sparking debates about national jurisdiction and international intervention. Negotiations and compromises were vital. The tribunal's establishment itself was a compromise, acknowledging the need for international justice while respecting, to a degree, Rwandan sovereignty. However, the trial process involved numerous complex issues, including witness protection, evidence gathering amidst widespread trauma, and ensuring fair trials in the face of considerable societal upheaval. These challenges highlighted the practical difficulties of applying international criminal justice principles within a context of deep-seated national trauma and ongoing political sensitivities. The balance between ensuring accountability and safeguarding national sovereignty proved incredibly difficult to achieve.

The International Criminal Tribunal for the former Yugoslavia (ICTY), established in 1993, faced similar, yet distinct, challenges. Unlike the ICTR, which dealt with a concentrated period of violence, the ICTY addressed a prolonged conflict characterized by complex ethnic tensions and shifting political landscapes. The ICTY's mandate covered a broader range of crimes, including war crimes, crimes against humanity, and genocide. Its operations involved navigating the complex political dynamics of the former Yugoslavia, including competing claims of sovereignty from newly independent states. The Tribunal's work was impacted by the ongoing political instability and the reluctance of some states to fully cooperate with its investigations and prosecutions. This led to significant delays and challenges in securing evidence and witness testimony, while the scope of its investigations often challenged the sensitivities of states emerging from the conflict. The ICTY's work demonstrated the complexities of prosecuting international crimes in a region grappling with post-conflict reconciliation and nation-building.

Contemporary examples further illuminate this complex interplay. The ongoing investigations by the International Criminal Court (ICC) in situations like Darfur, the Central African Republic, and Ukraine demonstrate a continuing struggle to balance state sovereignty and the imperative for international criminal justice. The ICC's reliance on state cooperation for investigations and prosecutions often leads to friction when states resist cooperation, citing concerns about national sovereignty or domestic political considerations. Furthermore, the ICC's jurisdiction is frequently challenged by states that argue the court's actions infringe upon their sovereign right to prosecute their own citizens. These situations underscore the delicate balancing act inherent in the pursuit of international justice while respecting the principle of state sovereignty. Negotiations, political pressure, and diplomatic efforts are often required to secure cooperation and overcome obstacles to justice, highlighting the continuing tension between these fundamental principles. The need for creative solutions and continuous dialogue remains essential.

The conflicts and compromises in these examples illustrate the inherent tensions between state sovereignty and international criminal justice. While the establishment of international tribunals and the ICC signifies a growing recognition of the need for international accountability for serious crimes, the reality is often far more nuanced. Successfully applying international criminal justice requires addressing individual state concerns about national sovereignty, while simultaneously ensuring justice for victims of atrocities. Finding practical and sustainable ways to reconcile these competing interests is a key challenge for the international community. Effective international mechanisms must not only be legally sound but also politically astute, sensitive to cultural contexts, and willing to engage in flexible negotiations to ensure successful outcomes. The pursuit of justice must be pursued alongside respectful engagement with state sovereignty, recognizing the need for collaborative and mutually beneficial partnerships.

Ultimately, a robust international criminal justice system depends on a balance between the universal principles of justice and the legitimate concerns of states regarding their sovereignty. The path forward demands ongoing dialogue, creative compromise, and a willingness to adapt strategies to address the unique challenges posed by each case. International cooperation, including mutual respect for states' capacities and limitations, alongside continued efforts to enhance international legal instruments and practices, will be crucial to successfully navigating the complex and evolving field of international criminal justice. It is a delicate dance, one that demands both firmness in upholding justice and sensitivity to preserving the integrity and independence of nations. Only through such a delicate balance can a true and lasting harmony between justice and sovereignty be achieved.

5.1 Rwanda Genocide Tribunal

The Rwandan Genocide, a horrifying event etched in the annals of history, necessitated a unique approach to international justice. The sheer scale of the atrocities, the complete breakdown of the Rwandan state's capacity to prosecute the perpetrators, and the urgency to bring those responsible to account, led to the creation of the International Criminal Tribunal for Rwanda (ICTR). Unlike the ad hoc tribunals that preceded it, the ICTR's establishment showcased a growing international consensus on the necessity of addressing mass atrocities regardless of the political complexities involved. Its mandate was clear: to prosecute those responsible for genocide, crimes against humanity, and war crimes committed during the 1994 genocide. This wasn't simply about retribution; it was about seeking truth, ensuring accountability, and ultimately, fostering reconciliation within a deeply scarred nation.

The ICTR faced significant challenges, however. Many of the accused initially evaded capture, highlighting the complexities of international arrest warrants and the need for robust cooperation from states. Securing evidence from a devastated country, many witnesses deeply traumatized, and a justice system already in disrepair, proved formidable. Moreover, the sheer volume of cases demanded an extensive logistical operation, requiring significant financial and personnel resources from the international community. While the UN provided funding and support, resource constraints consistently hindered the tribunal's efforts, prolonging trials and delaying justice for the victims. This underscored the practical limitations of establishing international tribunals, particularly in post-conflict environments where the very infrastructure needed for a functioning justice system lay in ruins.

One critical aspect of the ICTR was its reliance on international law and human rights principles. The tribunal meticulously adhered to international legal standards, ensuring due process rights for the accused while simultaneously holding them accountable for their heinous crimes. The ICTR's judgments, despite limitations, contributed significantly to the evolving international legal framework for prosecuting genocide and similar atrocities. Indeed, the ICTR's jurisprudence helped clarify various legal definitions, providing crucial precedents for future prosecutions of similar crimes. This development was crucial in solidifying the principle that state sovereignty does not shield individuals from international criminal accountability.

However, the ICTR's legacy is complex. While successful in convicting high-ranking officials, it also faced criticism regarding its slow pace, high costs, and challenges in effectively engaging with the local Rwandan community. This raised important questions regarding the balance between international justice mechanisms and the needs of the affected population. Some argued that the ICTR failed to adequately address the issue of reparations for victims, and that traditional justice mechanisms, albeit imperfect, could have played a more significant role in reconciliation efforts. This debate highlights the challenges of integrating international criminal justice with national reconciliation processes in post-conflict settings.

The ICTR's impact extended beyond the courtroom. Its existence signaled a growing international commitment to end impunity for serious human rights violations. It fostered a sense of accountability, albeit a delayed one, for the perpetrators, sending a powerful message that even state-sponsored violence would not go unpunished. The tribunal's work also laid the groundwork for the International Criminal Court (ICC), which subsequently built upon the lessons learned from the ICTR and other ad hoc tribunals. The ICTR, despite its imperfections, remains a crucial turning point in the evolution of international criminal justice. Its existence marked a significant departure from traditional understandings of state sovereignty, demonstrating the growing willingness of the international community to intervene in matters of grave human rights abuses, even within the boundaries of a nation's territory. The tribunal's legacy continues to shape the ongoing debate regarding the interplay between state sovereignty and international justice, underscoring the inherent complexities and challenges in achieving true accountability while respecting the principle of national sovereignty. This delicate balance continues to be a focus of international legal development and future efforts to prevent and prosecute atrocity crimes. The ICTR's experience serves as a valuable case study, rich with lessons for navigating the complex relationship between sovereignty and the pursuit of justice in the global arena.

5.2 Yugoslavia Tribunal

The International Criminal Tribunal for the former Yugoslavia (ICTY), established in 1993, represented a landmark attempt to reconcile state sovereignty with the imperative of international justice. Its mandate, stemming from UN Security Council resolutions, directly challenged the traditional notion of absolute state sovereignty by asserting the international community's right to prosecute individuals for serious crimes committed within a state's borders, even without that state's explicit consent. This unprecedented assertion, born from the horrors of the Yugoslav Wars, involved navigating a complex legal and political landscape. The Tribunal's establishment marked a significant departure from the historical precedent of states solely holding jurisdiction over crimes committed within their territory.

Its creation was a direct response to the widespread atrocities committed during the conflicts in the former Yugoslavia, including genocide, war crimes, and crimes against humanity. The sheer scale of the crimes, coupled with the apparent inability or unwillingness of the involved states to bring perpetrators to justice, galvanized international action. The ICTY became a powerful symbol of the international community's determination to hold individuals accountable for such egregious violations of international humanitarian law, regardless of their status or the sovereignty claims of their nation-states. The Tribunal's existence demonstrated a clear shift in the global understanding of state responsibility and the limits of national jurisdiction in cases of widespread human rights abuses.

However, the ICTY's operation was not without its challenges. Its legitimacy, particularly among the states of the former Yugoslavia, was frequently questioned. Accusations of bias, political interference, and the prosecution of individuals from certain groups more frequently than others, fueled resistance and skepticism. These criticisms, although often politically motivated, highlight the inherent difficulties of establishing a truly impartial international court operating within a politically charged environment. The challenges faced by the ICTY underscored the difficulties of balancing the principles of justice with the sensibilities of sovereign states, particularly when dealing with recent conflicts and deeply entrenched nationalist sentiment.

The Tribunal's prosecutors faced significant obstacles in gathering evidence, securing the cooperation of witnesses, and overcoming the challenges of navigating conflicting national laws and jurisdictions. Many witnesses, fearing for their safety or influenced by national loyalties, hesitated to testify. Securing the arrest and transfer of indicted individuals also posed significant problems, highlighting the limitations of international law enforcement mechanisms and the critical role of state cooperation in ensuring the ICTY's effectiveness. The process often faced delays, further exacerbating frustration among victims and raising concerns about the overall efficiency of the Tribunal. Successful prosecutions were often hampered by these various obstacles.

Despite its limitations and controversies, the ICTY left an undeniable legacy. Its work contributed significantly to the development of international criminal law, clarifying the definitions of various international crimes and establishing precedents for future prosecutions. The ICTY's jurisprudence and procedural innovations served as a blueprint for other international tribunals, notably the International Criminal Tribunal for Rwanda (ICTR) and, eventually, the International Criminal Court (ICC). The body of case law developed by the ICTY significantly informed the evolution of international legal norms concerning state sovereignty and individual accountability for heinous crimes. Its legacy can be found within the framework of numerous future prosecutions.

Furthermore, the ICTY's focus on individual criminal responsibility, rather than solely on state responsibility, represented a notable shift in the international legal landscape. This shift fundamentally altered the understanding of accountability for gross human rights violations and laid the foundation for a more comprehensive approach to international justice. Its efforts towards accountability, coupled with the recognition of individual crimes, regardless of national borders, made a substantial contribution to ongoing efforts toward fostering a world where such atrocities are less likely to occur. The Tribunal's impact extended beyond the courtroom, serving as a catalyst for broader debates about transitional justice, reconciliation, and the role of international law in addressing past atrocities.

The ICTY's experience serves as a valuable case study in the ongoing tension between state sovereignty and international criminal justice. It illustrates the complexities of enforcing international norms in the face of national resistance, highlighting the necessity for robust international cooperation and the importance of balancing the pursuit of justice with the need to respect state sovereignty. The tribunal's successes and failures provided crucial lessons for the design and operation of subsequent international criminal justice mechanisms, ultimately contributing to a more refined and sophisticated approach to international justice. The legacy of the ICTY continues to shape the landscape of international law and the ongoing global pursuit of accountability for mass atrocities. Its complexities serve as a stark reminder of the challenges inherent in the delicate balancing act between sovereign nations and a collective desire for justice.

5.3 Contemporary Examples

The ongoing conflict in Ukraine vividly illustrates the contemporary tension between state sovereignty and international criminal justice. Russia's invasion, its alleged war crimes, and the subsequent investigations by international bodies like the ICC highlight the limitations of existing mechanisms. While the principle of state sovereignty protects national interests, the scale of atrocities necessitates a robust international response, creating a significant challenge to the traditional notion of exclusive national jurisdiction. The international community's attempts to hold perpetrators accountable face numerous obstacles, ranging from political maneuvering to practical difficulties in gathering evidence and securing cooperation from relevant states. This case demonstrates the complexities inherent in balancing the need for justice with the deeply held principle of state self-determination.

The situation in Syria presents a different, yet equally compelling, example. The ongoing civil war and the alleged use of chemical weapons have prompted various international investigations and calls for accountability. However, the fragmented nature of the conflict, the involvement of multiple actors, and the lack of a unified international consensus on how to proceed have hampered efforts to establish a clear path towards justice. While some states have pursued individual prosecutions based on universal jurisdiction, others have prioritized their own national interests and security concerns, ultimately hindering the establishment of an effective international justice framework. The Syrian case highlights the practical challenges of securing international co-operation and the political complexities involved in navigating competing national interests.

Consider the ongoing debate surrounding the prosecution of individuals for crimes against humanity and war crimes committed in the context of the Israeli-Palestinian conflict. Here, the deeply entrenched political divide and the competing narratives surrounding the conflict have complicated the pursuit of international justice. The establishment of international mechanisms to investigate and prosecute alleged crimes has been met with resistance and strong objections from both sides, with each side maintaining that their actions are justified within the context of their legitimate self-defense. This situation underscores the immense political difficulties involved in achieving international justice in highly charged political contexts, where accusations and counter-accusations become intertwined with deeply held national identities and historical grievances. Progress towards accountability necessitates finding a way to overcome these divisions and establish impartial mechanisms for investigating allegations, something currently lacking.

The Rohingya crisis in Myanmar exemplifies another complex scenario where state sovereignty directly clashes with the demand for international justice. The widespread allegations of genocide and crimes against humanity against the Myanmar military have met with limited international response, despite strong condemnations and international reports documenting egregious human rights abuses. Myanmar's government has consistently resisted international pressure, citing national sovereignty and internal affairs as reasons for not cooperating with international inquiries. This highlights the limitations of international legal mechanisms when confronted with a state that actively rejects international intervention and maintains its own version of national legal processes, making international justice a formidable challenge. Such situations demand a careful and nuanced approach, seeking creative ways to secure justice without compromising the sovereignty of nations entirely.

The rise of non-state actors, including terrorist organizations and armed groups, poses another significant challenge to contemporary international criminal justice. The decentralized nature of these groups, their cross-border activities, and the absence of a clear state apparatus to be held accountable complicate the establishment of international justice mechanisms. Although several international tribunals and courts have successfully prosecuted members of non-state actors, many challenges remain, such as ensuring effective cooperation from states in apprehending and extraditing suspects. Furthermore, effective prosecution often requires extensive international cooperation and the willingness of various states to relinquish certain aspects of their national sovereignty in order to facilitate joint investigations and judicial proceedings. This underscores the need for flexible and adaptable legal frameworks that can address the unique challenges posed by non-state actors. The complexity lies in reconciling the protection of state sovereignty with the need for an effective international response to the global threat that these groups represent, balancing the security of nations and the pursuit of international justice.

6 The Future of International Criminal Justice

The International Criminal Court (ICC), while a landmark achievement, faces significant hurdles. Its effectiveness hinges heavily on the cooperation of states, a cooperation often lacking due to political considerations, national interests, and a reluctance to surrender sovereignty. Strengthening the ICC requires a multifaceted approach. This includes bolstering its investigative capacity, ensuring consistent financial support from member states, and developing clearer and more consistent legal frameworks to address procedural ambiguities. Furthermore, the ICC needs to enhance its communication and outreach strategies to foster greater public understanding and acceptance of its mandate and actions. Addressing criticisms fairly and transparently, while implementing necessary reforms, is crucial for its continued legitimacy and effectiveness. Ultimately, increased cooperation among states will be vital. This won't simply happen; it requires proactive engagement, including diplomatic initiatives, capacity-building programs aimed at strengthening national justice systems, and the development of robust mechanisms for information-sharing and coordination.

One promising avenue for enhanced cooperation lies in building stronger partnerships between the ICC and regional and national courts. Complementarity, the cornerstone of the ICC's relationship with national systems, must be actively promoted and strengthened. This entails providing technical and financial assistance to national courts to improve their capacity to investigate and prosecute international crimes. Joint investigations and prosecutions, when possible and appropriate, could foster trust and mutual understanding, leading to increased referrals to the ICC. Encouraging states to ratify and fully implement the Rome Statute remains a critical goal. The participation of more states not only strengthens the Court's legitimacy but also expands its reach, potentially leading to greater accountability for perpetrators of atrocities.

Balancing state sovereignty and the pursuit of international justice demands a nuanced and pragmatic approach. It's not a zero-sum game; rather, it's a complex interplay that demands constant negotiation and adaptation. Recognizing the legitimate concerns of states regarding their sovereignty is crucial. For instance, concerns regarding national security or the perceived threat to political stability could be addressed through mechanisms such as tailored cooperation agreements that respect states' legal frameworks and ensure their participation is voluntary and respects the principle of complementarity. Ultimately, the goal is a collaborative relationship, one that strengthens national systems while fostering broader accountability. The alternative—a world where impunity reigns—holds far greater risks to international peace and security.

The concept of universal jurisdiction provides an additional legal avenue for pursuing justice for serious international crimes. While controversial, its potential contribution to accountability in cases where the ICC lacks jurisdiction or cooperation is undeniable. However, the exercise of universal jurisdiction should be governed by principles of restraint, proportionality, and non-interference in the domestic affairs of other states. Transparency and close consultation with relevant states are crucial to ensure compliance with international law and avoid escalating tensions. Carefully defined jurisdictional standards, together with robust due process protections and adherence to fair trial principles, are essential for mitigating the risks of abuse.

Looking ahead, the future of international criminal justice will depend not only on the strength of international institutions but also on the commitment of states to uphold the rule of law and cooperate in the pursuit of justice. This requires a long-term investment in capacity building, conflict prevention, and education, as well as a consistent effort to promote a culture of accountability and respect for human rights globally. The challenge lies in finding a balance between preserving sovereignty and promoting universal justice, ensuring that neither principle overshadows the other. International cooperation is not merely a strategy for strengthening international institutions; it's the foundation upon which a system of just and effective international criminal justice must rest. This journey will require sustained efforts, a commitment to diplomacy, and a recognition of the inherent complexities involved. Only through such a sustained commitment can we hope to create a world where perpetrators of atrocity crimes are held accountable, without compromising the principles of state sovereignty.

6.1 Strengthening the ICC

The International Criminal Court (ICC), despite its commendable ambition, faces significant hurdles in effectively prosecuting perpetrators of international crimes. Its success hinges crucially on increased state cooperation, a challenge often framed as a conflict between national sovereignty and universal justice. Strengthening the ICC necessitates a multifaceted approach, moving beyond simplistic calls for compliance and engaging with the complex political realities that influence state behavior. A key starting point lies in fostering a more robust understanding and appreciation of the ICC's mandate among state actors. This requires targeted diplomatic engagement, tailored to the specific concerns and priorities of individual nations. Clear and consistent communication, emphasizing the ICC's role in upholding international law and deterring future atrocities, is paramount. We must move beyond generic pronouncements and engage in nuanced dialogues that address national security concerns, political sensitivities, and potential economic implications.

Effective strategies must consider the diverse capacities of states.

Providing technical assistance and capacity building programs to nations lacking the resources or expertise to engage with the ICC is vital. This assistance should extend beyond mere legal training, encompassing support for judicial reforms, witness protection programs, and the development of effective investigative capabilities. International collaboration on these initiatives, involving both developed and developing nations, can ensure broader participation and ownership. The emphasis should be on fostering partnerships rather than imposing obligations.

Furthermore, reforming the ICC's internal processes can significantly enhance its legitimacy and effectiveness. This includes streamlining its procedures to reduce delays and enhance efficiency, a particularly sensitive area for states concerned about protracted legal battles. Improving transparency and public communication about its activities, to ensure broader understanding and trust, is equally critical. Mechanisms to proactively engage with civil society and victims' groups, incorporating their insights into investigations and prosecutions, are crucial for maintaining the ICC's ethical and practical foundation. Critically, addressing criticisms regarding the ICC's focus and priorities is necessary to ensure its sustainable development. This involves engaging in an open dialogue with states that have expressed concerns about selectivity or perceived bias, seeking to establish a system of justice that operates fairly and consistently.

Financial sustainability remains a major concern. Exploring innovative mechanisms for securing funding, beyond reliance on state contributions alone, is essential. This could include the establishment of a dedicated international fund, supported by private donations, charitable organizations, or even the creation of a levy on international trade, to create sustainable support without compromising national interests. Securing these additional revenue streams will reduce the financial strain on states, helping to facilitate cooperation and increase the ICC's operational capacity. Ultimately, strengthening the ICC requires a shift in perspective. It's not merely about enforcing international law; it's about building trust and fostering a system of justice that is perceived as equitable and effective. This will require both internal reforms and sustained diplomatic engagement, a long-term commitment that involves carefully weighing national interests against the broader pursuit of universal justice. The challenge lies in crafting a system where the protection of state sovereignty and the pursuit of international justice are not mutually exclusive goals but rather complementary aspects of a more stable and peaceful international order. Only through such a holistic, nuanced approach can we hope to achieve lasting improvements in the ICC's capacity to effectively uphold justice for the victims of international crimes and prevent future atrocities. Building bridges of understanding between states and the ICC requires a continuous and collaborative effort, one that acknowledges diverse perspectives and prioritizes the long-term objective of a global justice system capable of bringing accountability to those who violate international law. The path forward requires a consistent commitment to dialogue, compromise, and building capacity, a journey that requires patience and the sustained dedication of all stakeholders.

6.2 State Cooperation Strategies

Effective state cooperation is paramount to the International Criminal Court's (ICC) success. Without it, the ICC remains a largely symbolic body, unable to fulfill its mandate of prosecuting perpetrators of grave international crimes. This necessitates a multifaceted approach, encompassing legal, political, and diplomatic strategies. The challenge lies in finding a balance that respects national sovereignty while simultaneously upholding the principles of international justice.

One crucial element involves strengthening the legal framework governing state cooperation. This means improving the clarity and precision of the Rome Statute, particularly regarding the obligations of states parties. Ambiguities must be addressed to prevent selective interpretation and non-compliance. Moreover, mechanisms for dispute resolution between the ICC and states should be reinforced, allowing for impartial arbitration in cases of disagreement. Robust enforcement mechanisms are also needed, including the possibility of targeted sanctions against states consistently failing to cooperate.

Diplomacy plays a vital role in encouraging state cooperation. The ICC's outreach efforts should be intensified, with a focus on building trust and understanding among reluctant states. This involves engaging in transparent and open dialogue, addressing concerns regarding national interests and sovereignty in a respectful and constructive manner. Targeted diplomatic initiatives, tailored to the specific context and concerns of individual states, are crucial. Incentivizing cooperation through capacity-building programs, technical assistance, and financial support can also significantly enhance willingness to participate.

Furthermore, political will is indispensable. The international community must exert pressure on states that obstruct the ICC's work. This pressure can take the form of targeted sanctions, diplomatic isolation, and public condemnation. However, such measures should be applied judiciously and transparently to avoid undermining international relations unnecessarily. Simultaneously, robust support for states willing to cooperate, perhaps through enhanced security partnerships or economic assistance, can create a positive feedback loop, encouraging broader compliance.

Beyond these immediate strategies, a longer-term approach is essential. This involves fostering a culture of accountability and respect for international law at the national level. This requires educational initiatives aimed at raising awareness among policy-makers, law enforcement officials, and the general public about the importance of international criminal justice and state cooperation. Judicial training programs can build capacity and expertise in prosecuting international crimes domestically, potentially reducing the reliance on the ICC for all cases.

Finally, exploring innovative approaches to cooperation, such as witness protection programs tailored to the specific cultural context of each country, is necessary. Moreover, investigating the creation of joint investigative teams, composed of both ICC and national investigators, can effectively enhance trust and efficiency while minimizing the perception of interference in national affairs. These joint teams could potentially leverage the expertise of both national and international actors, benefiting from their respective strengths. Careful consideration must be given to the sensitive balance between collaboration and upholding national sovereignty. Ultimately, sustained effort across all these fronts is key to enabling the ICC's full potential and achieving a world where impunity for atrocity crimes is a thing of the past. The pursuit of international justice and the preservation of national sovereignty are not mutually exclusive but rather two sides of the same coin, requiring careful and considered approaches for effective implementation.

6.3 Balancing Sovereignty and Justice

Finding equilibrium between state sovereignty and international criminal justice demands a nuanced approach. The inherent tension stems from the historical understanding of sovereignty as absolute authority within a state's borders, juxtaposed against the increasingly recognized need for universal accountability for egregious crimes that transcend national boundaries. This isn't about undermining national structures; instead, it's about recognizing that certain atrocities demand a response beyond the capacity—or perhaps the will—of individual nations.

Effective international criminal justice mechanisms necessitate a level of state cooperation that often clashes with deeply ingrained notions of national independence. States are understandably hesitant to cede authority over their citizens or to subject their officials to international scrutiny. This reluctance, however, often hinders the pursuit of justice for victims and perpetuates impunity for perpetrators of heinous crimes. The challenge lies in designing systems that respect the legitimate concerns of states while simultaneously ensuring that those responsible for atrocities are held accountable.

One crucial aspect is fostering a culture of mutual respect and understanding. International bodies and individual states need to engage in open and honest dialogue, recognizing the valid security concerns of states while stressing the importance of collective responsibility for addressing international crimes. This entails building trust, sharing information effectively, and collaboratively developing strategies that minimize the perceived threat to sovereignty while maximizing the potential for justice. Effective diplomacy is paramount; the use of coercive measures should be a last resort.

Furthermore, pragmatic solutions are needed. Perhaps the most promising path forward lies in strengthening the complementarity principle. This principle, already embedded in the Rome Statute of the International Criminal Court, suggests that the ICC should act as a court of last resort, intervening only when national courts are unwilling or unable to prosecute serious crimes. By emphasizing national courts' primary role, the ICC could alleviate some of the anxieties surrounding potential infringements on sovereignty. Strengthening national judicial capacities to investigate and prosecute such crimes is crucial. International assistance and training programs can help build these capabilities. Successful implementation requires a comprehensive approach. This involves strengthening international law, enhancing cooperation among states, and fostering a shared commitment to justice. It requires addressing issues of capacity building, resource allocation, and ensuring the independence and impartiality of international tribunals. Simultaneously, mechanisms for addressing legitimate state concerns regarding the ICC's jurisdiction and procedures need refinement. Transparent and predictable processes can help alleviate anxieties and encourage cooperation.

Ultimately, achieving a balance requires a shift in perspective. State sovereignty should not be seen as an absolute barrier to international justice but rather as a framework within which international cooperation for justice can flourish. A focus on shared responsibility, collaborative mechanisms, and capacity building will lead to a system that promotes accountability while respecting national interests. The goal isn't to eliminate state sovereignty; it's to adapt it to the realities of a globalized world where heinous crimes necessitate a global response. This requires a fundamental rethinking of international relations and a commitment to collaborative justice. Through ongoing dialogue and a commitment to practical solutions, a more harmonious future, one where sovereignty and justice coexist, can be achieved.

The path toward balancing sovereignty and justice is not without its obstacles. Political considerations, conflicting national interests, and resource constraints continue to pose significant challenges. However, by fostering open dialogue, strengthening international legal frameworks, and committing to pragmatic solutions, the international community can strive toward a more just and equitable world. This requires a long-term commitment to collaboration, diplomacy, and a shared recognition that the pursuit of justice transcends national borders and requires collective effort. The task is not simple, and progress may be gradual. Still, through persistent engagement and a spirit of cooperation, the world can move toward a future where sovereignty and justice are not mutually exclusive but complementary principles, essential to maintaining peace and security for all.

7 Conclusion: Towards a Harmonious Future

The journey through the complexities of state sovereignty and international criminal justice has revealed a dynamic interplay, a constant negotiation between the age-old principles of national autonomy and the burgeoning need for global accountability. We've witnessed the evolution from a predominantly state-centric system to one increasingly recognizing the imperative of prosecuting grave international crimes, regardless of national borders. This tension, however, is not insurmountable; rather, it presents an opportunity for innovative solutions and collaborative approaches.

The inherent challenges, as evidenced throughout our examination of the International Criminal Court, universal jurisdiction, and various case studies, are substantial. Resistance from states concerned about their sovereignty is a recurring theme, coupled with the practical difficulties of securing cooperation, gathering evidence across international borders, and ensuring fair trials within a complex legal framework. Yet, these obstacles are not insurmountable; indeed, they highlight the necessity for continuous refinement and adaptation. Successful prosecutions, like those at the International Criminal Tribunal for the former Yugoslavia and the International Criminal Tribunal for Rwanda, despite their limitations, offer valuable precedents and lessons learned.

Moving forward necessitates a pragmatic approach. The ICC, while not without flaws, represents a critical institution in the global effort to combat impunity. Its effectiveness hinges on strengthened cooperation among states, improvements in its internal processes, and a continued commitment to complementarity - a principle that acknowledges the primary role of national jurisdictions while allowing the ICC to step in when these fail. This delicate balance, the cornerstone of a harmonious future, demands meticulous negotiation, understanding, and a commitment to mutual respect.

Strengthening the ICC isn't merely a matter of increasing its budget or expanding its staff. It requires a fundamental shift in global attitudes towards international justice. This includes fostering a culture of accountability, where states see the prosecution of international crimes not as an affront to their sovereignty, but as a vital tool for preventing future atrocities and maintaining international peace and security. Educational initiatives, focused on fostering a deeper understanding of international law and the principles of international criminal justice, are essential. Furthermore, effective mechanisms for addressing state concerns regarding sovereignty, such as robust safeguards against political interference and transparent procedures, are needed.

The path toward a harmonious future demands a commitment to dialogue and collaboration. States must engage in good-faith negotiations, seeking common ground and recognizing the shared interest in preventing and punishing atrocities. This might involve developing more flexible mechanisms for state cooperation, creating specialized units within national judiciaries to handle international crimes, and streamlining evidence-sharing procedures. It may even involve exploring alternative forms of justice, such as restorative justice approaches, where appropriate, to address the underlying causes of conflict and promote reconciliation.

Ultimately, the reconciliation of state sovereignty and international criminal justice is not a zero-sum game. It is a process of continuous negotiation and adaptation, demanding creativity, compromise, and a shared vision for a world where justice prevails and the sovereignty of nations is respected within a framework of global responsibility. The future of international criminal justice lies in finding practical solutions that balance these competing, yet intertwined, interests. This requires a profound shift in mindset, one that embraces collaboration over confrontation, understanding over suspicion, and a commitment to building a truly just and harmonious international order. The challenges are significant, but the potential rewards - a safer, more accountable world - make the pursuit worthwhile. We stand at a crossroads, the choice is ours: continue down the path of conflict and fragmentation, or forge a new path, one of cooperation and shared responsibility, towards a future where sovereignty and justice coexist, not as adversaries, but as complementary pillars of a stable and peaceful international community.

7.1 Reconciliation Efforts

Successful reconciliation following mass atrocities requires a multifaceted approach, moving beyond mere legal processes. Genuine healing necessitates addressing the deep-seated trauma experienced by victims and communities. This includes providing access to comprehensive psychosocial support, ensuring avenues for truth-telling and remembrance, and facilitating processes of reparations for the harms suffered. These efforts are crucial, not only for individual healing but also for fostering social cohesion and preventing future violence. Effective reconciliation initiatives aren't just about punishing perpetrators; they're about rebuilding trust and fostering a sense of collective responsibility for creating a more just future.

The importance of transitional justice mechanisms, including truth commissions, cannot be overstated. These bodies provide platforms for victims to share their experiences, holding perpetrators accountable without necessarily relying solely on criminal prosecution. The Rwandan experience, though imperfect, demonstrates the potential of truth commissions to contribute significantly to reconciliation, promoting a deeper understanding of the events that led to the genocide and fostering a sense of shared history. However, their effectiveness is contingent upon factors such as political will, adequate resources, and a commitment to implementing their recommendations. These commissions must operate with complete transparency and impartiality, engaging with diverse communities to ensure inclusivity.

Furthermore, community-based reconciliation initiatives can play a crucial role. These locally driven efforts recognize the unique contexts and needs of specific communities, tailoring interventions to address local challenges. Grassroots programs focusing on dialogue, forgiveness, and community healing can build bridges between victims and perpetrators, fostering a sense of shared humanity. Such programs, while potentially resource-intensive, can be incredibly impactful, particularly in creating a safe and conducive environment for reconciliation at a community level. They might involve facilitating dialogue groups, providing conflict resolution training, and supporting community development projects.

Economic and social reconstruction are intrinsically linked to reconciliation. Addressing the socio-economic disparities that may have contributed to the conflict is crucial for preventing future violence and fostering stability. This necessitates investments in education, healthcare, infrastructure, and economic development. It also requires addressing issues of land ownership, property restitution, and access to resources. Sustainable development is not merely an economic imperative but a vital component of lasting reconciliation, ensuring that all members of the community have a chance to participate in the rebuilding process, which directly combats the underlying causes of conflict.

However, even with comprehensive efforts, reconciliation is a complex and protracted process. There will be challenges and setbacks along the way. The concept of transitional justice itself is constantly evolving and adapting to new circumstances; there's no single universally accepted blueprint. It requires sustained commitment, flexibility, and a willingness to learn from past experiences. International support, while essential, should be tailored to the specific needs of the affected nation, avoiding imposing external models or solutions that may not be culturally appropriate or sustainable in the long term. Respect for national ownership and local capacity building is key for lasting success. Ultimately, reconciliation is not simply an end goal but a continuous process. It demands ongoing commitment from both individuals and institutions. It's about fostering a culture of respect, accountability, and human rights, ensuring that the lessons learned from past atrocities are applied to prevent future violations. The journey toward reconciliation is not linear; it involves navigating challenges and adapting to evolving circumstances. It requires a long-term perspective and sustained commitment to creating a more just and equitable society. The aim is not to erase the past but to learn from it, to acknowledge the suffering endured, and to build a future where such horrors are never repeated. This demands constant vigilance, education, and a commitment to human rights, ensuring that the voices of victims are heard and their needs addressed, paving the way for lasting peace and healing.

7.2 Looking Ahead

The path forward necessitates a nuanced approach, recognizing the inherent complexities. Simply demanding increased state co-operation without addressing underlying concerns risks further alienation and undermining the legitimacy of the international criminal justice system. We must acknowledge the legitimate security and political anxieties of states, especially those facing internal instability or external threats. Engaging in open dialogue, building trust, and providing tailored support are crucial to fostering genuine cooperation. This might include capacity building assistance for national judicial systems, enabling them to effectively prosecute international crimes, thereby reducing the need for external intervention.

A key element of future progress lies in strengthening the ICC's legitimacy and effectiveness. This includes improving its efficiency, transparency, and accountability mechanisms. A more robust and responsive court will inspire greater confidence among states and encourage broader participation. Careful consideration must be given to the fair representation of diverse perspectives within the ICC's structures, ensuring impartiality and preventing perceptions of bias. Furthermore, ensuring a predictable and consistent application of international law is paramount in upholding the rule of law globally. Inconsistency only erodes the system's credibility.

The complementarity principle, while vital in respecting state sovereignty, requires careful recalibration. It should neither be interpreted so strictly as to render the ICC ineffective, nor so loosely as to undermine national judicial processes. This requires a clearer articulation of the responsibilities of both the ICC and national courts, a framework that acknowledges both their jurisdiction and their shared goal of upholding justice. The development of joint investigation mechanisms and a streamlined information-sharing process between the ICC and national authorities would promote effective cooperation and improve overall efficiency.

Beyond the ICC, exploring alternative mechanisms to address transitional justice is essential. Truth commissions, reparations programs, and other forms of restorative justice can provide effective avenues for accountability, reconciliation, and healing, without necessarily infringing on state sovereignty in the same way as criminal prosecutions. They offer a more culturally sensitive approach in dealing with mass atrocities and offer a practical solution to the limitations of pure criminal justice approaches. Understanding the specific contexts within each nation-state will facilitate the tailoring of such solutions and encourage more meaningful cooperation.

Looking further ahead, we need to consider the growing influence of non-state actors in perpetrating international crimes. Terrorist groups, transnational criminal organizations, and other non-state entities operate beyond the traditional boundaries of state sovereignty, posing a significant challenge to existing international frameworks. This requires innovative approaches to international cooperation, including increased intelligence sharing between states, the development of stronger international legal instruments to address crimes committed by non-state actors and possibly the creation of specialized international tribunals to deal with these specific challenges.

Ultimately, the successful reconciliation of state sovereignty with international criminal justice demands a continuous process of dialogue, compromise, and adaptation. It requires a delicate balancing act between upholding the principle of national self-determination and ensuring that egregious violations of human rights do not go unpunished. It is not a destination but a journey, requiring ongoing commitment from states, international organizations, and civil society actors alike. This endeavor is crucial not only for holding perpetrators accountable but also for building a more just and stable international order. Failure to meet this challenge will only lead to continued impunity, hindering efforts towards lasting peace and reconciliation globally. The road ahead requires collective commitment, nuanced understanding and a long-term strategic vision. Only then can we approach a more harmonious future where the pursuit of justice does not overshadow the significance of state sovereignty and vice versa. The long-term objective is a world where justice is not just attainable but is also viewed as an intrinsic aspect of a sovereign nation's integrity and stability, not its antithesis.